Fun and Free (or almost Free) Dating Ideas
By Jean Young

EXPERIENCE
EVERYTHING
P U B L I S H I N G

Disclaimer

This document is geared towards providing exact and reliable information in regards to the topic and issue covered. The publication is sold with the idea that the publisher is not required to render accounting, officially permitted, or otherwise, qualified services. If advice is necessary, legal or professional, a practiced individual in the profession should be ordered.

- From a Declaration of Principles which was accepted and approved equally by a Committee of the American Bar Association and a Committee of Publishers and Associations:

The information provided herein is stated to be truthful and consistent, in that any liability, in terms of inattention or otherwise, by any usage or abuse of any policies, processes, or directions contained within is the solitary and utter responsibility of the recipient reader. Under no circumstances will any legal responsibility or blame be held against the publisher for any reparation, damages, or monetary loss due to the information herein, either directly or indirectly.

The information herein is offered for informational purposes solely, and is universal as so. The presentation of the information is without contract or any type of guarantee assurance.

The trademarks that are used are without any consent, and the publication of the trademark is without permission or backing by the trademark owner. All trademarks and brands within this book are for clarifying purposes only and are the owned by the owners themselves, not affiliated with this document.

Introduction

Fun Activities To Do With Your Partner Without Spending Money

Conclusion

Introduction

In the busy world that we live in today, there are so many things that can distract us from spending some quality time with our partners. We have our careers, family, sports and other extracurricular activities. We can't help but wish for more hours in the day so that we can do everything that we want to do and spend time with the people we want to spend time with. Because of the many distractions around us, it is normal to see couples spending less and less time with each other.

Married couples or those with kids often say that their family and being good parents is most important to them. However, it is ironic to see them spending less time with each other and setting aside their relationship. In order for couples to be the good parents that they want to be, couples need to have a happy relationship, a relationship where they are able to spend time with each other and are content with each other. For a family to be strong, the relationship of the couple has to be strong and solid too because that is going to be the foundation of the family.

Unfortunately, when couples spend less time together, they are also decreasing the chances of making a marriage or relationship work. When you spend time with your partner, you are also saving for the rainy days. It is easier for couples to overcome difficult situations when they have been spending time together. Couples are increasing the distance between them when they do not spend enough quality time together and the chances of hearing the words '*I don't love you anymore*' are greater.

You often hear couples saying that they are very much aware that they should be spending quality time with each other as soon as things slow down or settle. But if you are waiting for that to happen, then you are waiting for something that is never going to happen. Life won't slow down and something is always going to need to be taken care of. There could be meetings to go to, parties to attend, a homework that needs to be checked, or a sick child that needs to be taken to the doctor. The list of possible things that need immediate attention could go on and on.

Which leads us to the next question: why is it so difficult to spend quality time with our partners if it is very important? The common reason that you would hear is that they do not have enough resources (time or money) to go on a romantic vacation for two. Maybe this sounds familiar to you to. But guess what? Spending quality time with your partner does not need to be expensive. You don't even have to spend money if you are creative or resourceful enough.

You need to remember that you chose to be with your partner and spending time with your partner should be taken as a priority and not kept at the sidelines. It will be your partner who will make difficult situations tolerable and your partner can easily brighten the gloomy day that you just had. When you find ways to make it happen, it is always possible to spend some time with your partner. You do not have to spend hours at a time. Even several minutes can make a huge difference to your relationship.

Relationships will never be as simple as 1,2,3. But when you are more affectionate towards your partner and you let your partner feel that you truly love them, then you can certainly expect to have somebody to be by your side even when the path seems quite bumpy.

Fun Activities To Do With Your Partner Without Spending Money

When we mention spending quality time with our partners, we automatically think of out-of-town vacations or fancy dates. This can be a problem for people who have tight budgets. But don't fret because quality time with your partner does not have to be expensive. There are so many things that you can do that will not require you to spend a single cent.

As we mentioned earlier, when couples have kids already or have busy careers, it is quite easy to stop spending quality time with your partner in order to make more time for other things. This is not really a good idea. Did you know that even just a few minutes of quality time with your partner on a daily basis is already enough to bring good benefits for your relationship?

For example, before you head out to work spend a few minutes with your partner. Give your partner a goodbye kiss and hug. It will certainly help you go through the events that the day has in store for you. And when you or your partner comes back home from work, spend a few minutes with your partner to just talk about how the day went. In this way, your partner won't feel left out in the family.

Staying connected to your partner is also an important thing to keep the relationship in a great shape. When you and your partner are not together, it is important that you send messages to them just to let them know that you are thinking about them. No matter how busy the day is, do not let a day end without asking about how their day went. Open communication lines is a good way to keep couples connected.

Try to find time as well to take a look at each other's schedule for the upcoming week and use this time to discuss and set expectations. If you are going to be busy in the next few days because of meetings and other important things, it would be a great idea to inform your partner ahead of time so that their expectations are set and any plans for quality time in the next few days can be worked in the schedule too.

If you and your partner have a misunderstanding or something that's setting a bad vibe between you two, it is really important that you find the time to discuss it. Do not settle for not discussing issues and moving on as if nothing happened. These things tend to pile up and it will end up blowing up in your faces. You definitely do not want that.

And no matter how busy you are, whether it be with your career, your kids, or any other things that are keeping you preoccupied, it is still important that you and your partner find time to do something fun at least once a week to keep the spark going in your relationship. If your schedules allow date nights to happen more than once a week then that would be even better. Do not think that date nights have to be expensive in order for it to be fun. There are so many activities there that are free but fun for date nights anyway.

If you need more ideas for fun but free, or nearly free, things to do with your partner then keep on reading!

Tip #1: Surprise Dinner Date
You do not need to go to a fancy restaurant for a wonderful dinner date. Surprise your partner with a dinner date right at home, in your own kitchen. All you need to do is believe in that inner gourmet chef in you. Scavenge through your cupboards and fridge and see what you can come up with for dinner. To set a romantic mood, dim the lights and use candles. Once dinner is ready, take some time to dress yourself up. A bottle of wine is also a great way to give your dinner date at home a fancy touch!

Tip #2: Take Up A Sport
If you're into sporty activities, then maybe you should try out a sport with your partner. Maybe you have an old basketball lying around in your basement. Or how about taking out your pair of skates and heading to the skating rink with your partner. There are many different options for this one. Sometimes you do not really need to love what you are doing but rather enjoy it because you are doing it with someone that you love spending time with.

Tip #3: Use Your Talents
Are you a wonderful sketch artist or a painter? Why not ask your partner to model for you? Make a portrait of them. Or how about taking out your guitar or piano and singing to your heart's content with your partner. Or maybe reading a poem that you wrote for your partner. Whatever talent you have, come up with an activity that you can incorporate your talent with and make it something that you can do with your partner.

Tip #4: Bedtime Stories
Who ever said that bedtime stories are just for kids? They're not although you probably would not want to be reading your partner the same bedtime stories you'd be reading to your kids. Try a sexy story instead and you're certainly setting up the mood for a hot and steamy night. Or how about making up funny stories for a good laugh with your partner? Your imagination is the limit here.

Tip #5: Video Games
Not too many would consider this as a good activity for quality time unless you and your partner happen to be gamers. But then on the other hand, try to come up with video games that you two enjoyed when you were younger. There should be a video game or two that you both used to enjoy.

Tip #6: Movie Night

No need to go to the theater for a movie night because you can do it right at home. Do you have a DVD of a movie you want to watch again? Or maybe browse the channels on cable TV or Netflix and see if you can find something that you and your partner find interesting. To make sure that you stay snuggled to each other throughout the duration of the movie, make sure that you have snacks and drinks right within your reach.

Tip #7: Bath Time

Yes, adults can give each other baths too. It's definitely a sexy and intimate way to spend quality time together. You'll be helping each other unwind from the daily stress of life and you get to pamper each other too. Now doesn't that sound interesting?

Tip #8: Pillow Fights

Nobody is ever too old for anything, even pillow fights. So take some time off from being the serious you and entertain your partner with a pillow fight to bring out the inner kids in you two. But you need to remember that the idea here is to have a great night and not smash your partner too hard so be careful and cautious.

Tip #9: Free Concerts

If your town has a website or a page on a social network, you might want to check out the different activities that are scheduled to see if you can find anything that you and your partner might be interested in. You should also check out the calendars of towns near yours. You will be surprised to see that there are free entertainment scheduled every now and then.

Tip #10: Read Books

Reading books is fun but sometimes, people shy away from it when they need to purchase the book because of the cost. But don't worry. You and your bookworm partner can still enjoy good books at the library. Visit your local library. You should also know that there are many free activities offered at the library that are completely free like book clubs.

Tip #11: Listen To Podcasts

Okay, this is not everyone's kind of fun but it's certainly a good form of entertainment and a great source of knowledge too. There are so many interesting podcasts out there and the good things are they are for free and if you are not into reading books then you might just want to listen to one together and discuss.

Tip #12: Board Games

Now who doesn't love board games? We all have some kind of board game somewhere in our house. It's time to take them out and play with them. Although some board games may seem a little too childish or boring for our tastes, we can always put some twists in the game to make it more fun. You could maybe trying having a consequence for the loser of the game.

Tip #13: Make Bread

The things that you need for baking a loaf of bread are probably in your kitchen already. Why not have your partner help you out in measuring the ingredients for the bread which you can enjoy later when it's done? And you don't need to be experts to make bread. You just need a guide, ingredients, and your average baking supplies.

Tip #14: Learn How To Juggle

It is definitely fun to learn how to juggle. It can be frustrating but when your partner is learning with you, it is bound to be fun. And instead of getting frustrated, it is easy to laugh about your failed attempts. It is definitely a fun way to spend what could be a boring afternoon with your partner.

Tip #15: Clean Your House

Whoever said that cleaning can't be fun, they are definitely wrong. Put on upbeat tunes on loudspeaker and go through the things in your house with your partner. Sort out the things that needs to be thrown out and which ones should be kept. Coming across different things that remind you of something with your partner is a good way to recall memories that you and your partner had in the past. Go through your closets and maybe you will find the clothes you wore on your first date or maybe during your honeymoon. Then you and your partner will certainly be going down memory lane in no time.

Tip #16: Cupboard Potluck

What is this exactly? Invite your friends over for potluck dinner. But there is a twist in this plot. The special rule is that the ingredients of the food to be brought from dinner must come only from the things that you have in your cupboards and fridge. It's a good way to practice you and your partner's creativity and you and your partner will be rewarded with a night spent well with good friends.

Tip #17: Go On Your Own Guided Tour Of Your Place

Take the chance to look up the different historical events that happened in your place. Or maybe just some random interesting facts like a movie being shot at the town square. You can go to the library for details or look online. After learning the historic and interesting events that happened in your area, start organizing a tour of your place. Once everything is all set, then go on that tour that you organized with your partner. You could walk around the place or go for a drive if the places you want to show your partner are too far apart.

Tip #18: Be Photographers

Taking pictures can be done anytime anywhere these days. You only need to take out your digital camera or even your phone in order for you to start taking pictures. Go out for the day with the intention of taking pictures of the things that you walk by during the day or anything that catches your fancy. Take a stolen photo of your partner enjoying something that he likes or maybe take pictures of you two together. It is a good way to capture the memories that you have enjoyed during the day. And if your partner is also taking stolen shots of you, you are bound to be amazed by the different photos that he can capture. When you go home, reviewing the photos you have taken is a good way to reminisce the day you just spent together.

Tip #19: Blogging

If you and/or your partner are fond of writing, maybe the two of you would find it interesting to start your own blog and write about something that interests you and your partner. You could write blogs about the things that you do together, relationship advice and so on. There are quite a lot of websites out there that offer free blog service and they are not hard to get started and running either.

Tip #20: Museum Or Zoo Visit

There are actually some cities and even colleges that provide great yet free attractions that are also educational like zoos or museums. However, not all cities have this option. Check out if there are any times of the month that the museum, zoo or other educational attractions in your area that provide free or discounted admission.

Tip #21: Make A Video That You Can Upload Online

Think of something that you want to share with other internet users. It could be an instructional video, discussing a certain topic, making a spoof of a movie, a wonderful moment that you shared together and so on. You do not need much for this. Just come up with a concept for the video with your partner and use a video recorder or even a smartphone to record it and then upload it online. You could even use software for video editing to make the video more interesting.

Tip #22: Time Capsule

How do you do this? You and your partner could contribute things to your time capsule. Gather things that remind you of your relationship at the moment. You could make letters for each other or maybe make a video placed in a CD or flash drive that you can watch later when you open the box. Other things you could include could be a souvenir from your last date, plans for your future and so on. Once you have everything in the box, seal it and label it with the date you will be opening the box together. Then find a place to keep the box in. Make sure that the place is safe from the rain and other harmful things that could damage the box and its contents.

Tip #23: Share Old Photos/Videos

Surely you have a box or container somewhere that contains photos of you when you were younger and surely your partner has one too. Grab your own stash of old photos and spend a night sharing your stash to each other. It's a good way to get to know each other more especially the side of your partner prior to meeting them or being with them. And it is also a wonderful way to discover funny or hilarious things about each other.

Tip #24: Have Some Sexy Time

Oh yes. Nothing is more fun than finding different ways to seduce your partner and trying them out. What is even better is that it is totally free and it is a good way to turn up your creativity. You'll certainly get a great workout too from making out and doing the deed with your partner. Plus it will bring you closer to each other. If you have any worries or problems that you had prior to seducing your partner will be forgotten too and all is well once again between you two.

Tip #25: Yard Sale

This activity does not require you any money at all. But what is even better is that you actually have a shot at making money from things that you do not need or use anymore. Another bonus is that you will be clearing out your house of these unwanted items which can lead up to a clutter-free and more organized house. It is not hard to organize one either. To get the things that you want to put up for sale, you only need to go through your things with your partner and decide which ones you'd like to sell. Decide on the day that you want to have the yardsale, weekends would be more preferable. So where's the fun in having a yard sale when it sounds like so much has to be done to get it organized? You and your partner have the chance of mingling with your neighbors and enjoying the warm weather together.

Tip #26: Learn A New Foreign Language

You and your partner can embark on the journey of learning a new language together. Which language are both of you interested in learning? Once you've decided on that, it is time to start your lessons. And there is no need for the two of you to enroll in a class. There are many ways for you to learn a new language without having to pay for a tutor. There are online resources and there are apps that you can download in your phone or tablet. Learning should be more fun with your partner. You two can try having a conversation in the foreign language you are learning, watch movies, quiz each other or just have a friendly competition on who would be able to learn the language faster.

Tip #27: Volunteer

There are so many organizations out there that need only a volunteer's time to get things done. Look up some organizations that you and your partner might be interested in joining. A weekend spent doing volunteer work is a weekend spent well. You and your partner will have the chance of meeting other people that have different but interesting stories.

Tip #28: Have Fun With The Sprinklers

How about some quality time with your partner and your kids? Do you have water sprinklers in your garden? Time to turn them on and just run around the yard with your kids and partner getting wet. Even though the kids are around, you will surely get a few minutes alone with your partner since they'll probably be too busy playing with the water. It's a good way for the whole family to bond as well. Don't have kids? You can still do this activity! Maybe try throwing some water balloons at each other too!

Tip #29: Workout

As they always say, *'partners that workout together, stay together'*. Motivate each other to stay in a much better shape. Although you should not be telling your partner that he needs to lose some weight or else you'll be leaving them. That's definitely not a good idea. What you can tell your partner instead is that working out means you both will stay healthier. Or maybe you can tell them that if you both stay in shape, it might be easier for you to do that exotic sex position that you heard about or saw online the other night. Now that's a good motivator right there! But seriously, workouts are fun and they keep you healthy and working out with somebody makes the routine tolerable if you happen to be weary of such things.

You do not need to be enrolled in the gym for you and your partner to enjoy a good workout. There are so many routines out there that do not require any equipment at all. If you need help in putting together a workout routine for you and your partner, you can always check online for help. You'll surely find tons of videos and articles about workout routines that can be of great help.

Tip #30: Start A Journal

To start a journal, you only need a notebook and a pen and then some free time to write things in your journal. How do you get your partner involved in this? The two of you could write a journal addressed to each other where you will be able to share the things that you did for the day, your thoughts and if there are things that you need to tell your partner but do not have the guts to say face to face. Then set a time when you both will sit down and exchange journals. If you are up for it, you could discuss things that need to be discussed or maybe just write a reply to the other's journal entry. Yes, it does seem like there is a lack of privacy but you do not really need to write down things that you absolutely do not want your partner to know about. The journal is just intended for things you want to share to your partner but do not have the time or are too embarrassed to say out loud.

Tip #31: Write A Song Together

And why not? What makes it fun is it is a song that both of you have written together based on your experiences from the relationship, how you feel for each other and maybe even your hopes for the future. It is also a good reminder of how you felt for each other at the time that the song was composed. You do not need to be song writing experts.

Tip #32: Plan Your Next Vacation

You might not have the money now but you can always save up for your next vacation. While you are sitting on the porch or something, why not come up with ideas of how you want your next vacation to be. Imagine yourselves in the places you want to visit and the things that you want to do. Using your imagination is always a fun thing and planning your next vacation ahead of time gives you enough time to gather the necessary resources to make the vacation a reality.

Tip #33: Go On A Walk With No Particular Direction

This is another good way to get some exercise and you do not need to spend any money on this. To take your walk around the neighborhood with your partner, do not have a destination in mind. Instead, take directions that seem to be most interesting to the two of you and see where you end up at. Pretend to be tourists in the area if you wish and go at a pace that's most comfortable for the two of you. It's a great to have a catch-up conversation too especially if the two of you have been quite busy lately.

Tip #34: Massage Each Other

After a long and tiring day doing house chores or spending the day at work, would it not be nice to get a massage to loosen up your muscles and ease your mind? Massages are certainly great at helping one relax. Ask your partner to give you a massage. And you can also return the favor by giving them a massage as well.

Tip #35: Picnics

The sun is out and spending the day indoors seems like a waste of time. What should you and your partner do? Why not pack a basket of food and drinks taken right from your own kitchen and a towel or blanket to sit on then head on out for a picnic? You could go to the park, the beach or park some place that seems like a good spot for a picnic. Spend the day talking with your partner and enjoying the wonderful sunny day. And if you are headed out to the beach, might as well pack swimming suits for a quick swim to make the day even better.

Tip #36: TV Series Marathon

Is there a TV series that both of you and your partner like to watch but have not had the chance to watch it because of your busy schedules? Well, lucky for you there are online resources that will allow you to catch up on the series you like and what's even better is that they are ad free and you can watch them whenever you like. So if the weather won't permit you to stay outdoors but have nothing else to do indoors, why not watch the series online with your partner to pass the time away. Nothing is better than watching a series while having someone to cuddle up to, right?

Tip #37: Nature Hikes

Check your area for any nature hikes that you can go on with your partner. Pack your bags for things you might need like food, water, extra clothes and insect repellent and head on out to a trail. Take in the beauty of nature and find a spot to get some rest and enjoy the surrounding area.

Tip #38: Snowball Fights & Making A Snowman

It's winter and the snow is simply tempting. It is time for you and your partner to put on your warm clothes and enjoy the snow. And what's there to do in the snow? You could either have a snowball fight or make a snowman. Snowball fights will always be fun. But how about making a snowman? If you are feeling a little competitive, why not have a friendly competition on who would be able to make the cutest snowman. The loser has to face a consequence. Once done with your outdoor activity, you could head back indoors for a cup of hot chocolate and some cuddling time to make the cold go away.

Conclusion

For any relationship to work out and last for a long time, one of the most important things that couples must never forget is to spend some quality time together regularly. Not having money for a vacation or being too busy with whatever is keeping a person preoccupied is never an excuse for not spending time with the partner. In fact, if you really want something then you will always find ways to make what you want happen. Sometimes it might take a little effort but the result will be worth it because you are investing in your relationship.

There are many things that couples can actually do to have that quality time together. One does not need to go bankrupt in order for this to happen. It won't always be as romantic as how they show it in the movies but what's important is the effort and the fact that you and your partner exert to make sure having time for the other is a priority.

Aside from spending some quality time together, partners in a relationship should also have respect, trust and loyalty to each other for their relationship to work. And the efforts cannot come from one party alone but rather it should be a collective effort of the two people involved in the relationship.

EXPERIENCE
EVERYTHING
P U B L I S H I N G

www.ingramcontent.com/pod-product-compliance
Lightning Source LLC
Chambersburg PA
CBHW071812020426
42331CB00008B/2464